DATE DUE

SEP 0 2 1994		
JUN 1 0 1996		
FEB 2 6 2001		
GAYLORD		PRINTED IN U.S.A.

RUBBINGS AND TEXTURES

RUBBINGS AND TEXTURES

A Graphic Technique

John J. Bodor

Reinhold Book Corporation
A subsidiary of Chapman-Reinhold, Inc.
New York   Amsterdam   London
An Art Horizons Book

Frontispiece. Rubbing of King
Suryavarman II, the builder of Angkor Wat,
on his throne. Ink on paper. (Courtesy
the Weyhe Gallery, New York.)

Opposite Page
Rubbing by Robert S. Lindsley of the Stele
Raimondi from a prehistoric site in
Chavin, Peru. Ink on paper. (Courtesy
Eugene Fuller Memorial Collection, Seattle
Art Museum, Seattle, Washington.)

Also by the author:

Creating and Presenting Hand Puppets (Reinhold, 1967)

© 1968, Art Horizons, Inc.
All rights reserved
Printed in the United States of America
Library of Congress Catalog Card Number: 68-16026

Design Consultant: Milton Glaser
Type set by Graphic Arts Typographers, Inc.
Printed by New York Lithographing Corp.
Bound by William Marley Co.
Published by Reinhold Book Corporation
A subsidiary of Chapman-Reinhold, Inc.
430 Park Avenue, New York, N.Y. 10022

Contents

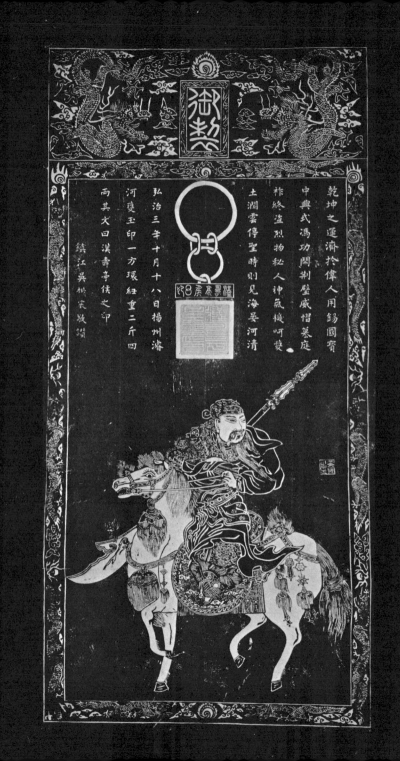

1.
A Brief History

"Rubbing" is a comparatively recent term for the ancient Chinese "ink squeeze" *(T'a-pen)* technique of copying engraved, carved or textured surfaces. A piece of paper is placed over the surface to be copied; the back of the paper is then "rubbed" with ink or other suitable material to produce a negative print. Thus, a rubbing of an image or calligraphy cut into a stone tablet appears as if executed with white ink on black paper.

While scholars agree that the technique had its birth in China, they have found it impossible to ascertain the exact time of its development. The earliest rubbing on paper to survive to the present day dates from the seventh century. It would, therefore, be reasonably safe to assume that the craft had its birth prior to this time, possibly as early as 300 B.C.

Although it never reached the prominence of wood engraving or painting, by the mid-fourteenth century the craft of rubbing had achieved a high level of technical and aesthetic perfection. Because rubbing was then, as it is today, primarily a means of reproduction, it never attained the status of a fine art. However, the practical role played by the technique was by no means minor. The practice of the craft was as wide spread as the boundaries of the Chinese empire. The need for a means of accurately disseminating the written word before the advent of the printing press was met through rubbing. Calligraphy was carved on stone tablets and displayed in metropolitan centers for all to see and copy. Pilgrims would interrupt their journeys long enough to take rubbings of the various stones. In this way much of the literature as well as edicts of the emperor were spread to the outermost frontiers of the empire. In addition to allowing the accurate copying of texts, rubbings preserved for centuries the calligraphic styles of the greatest scholars. Rubbing lent itself to this type of reproduction more than did wood engraving, which requires that texts and pictures be carved in reverse. Pictures were also carved in stone with the intent of their being copied. Again the rubbing technique, rather than wood engraving, was preferred, as there was no limitation as to size. There are many such pictures from the Ming and Ch'ing periods which further attest to the craft's popularity.

Perhaps the most outstanding and best-known rubbings are those taken from the series of sixteen Lo-han, or disciples of Buddha. The stone tablets were carved by order of emperor Ch'ien-lung in 1757 and are said to be copies of paintings executed by the Ch'an Buddhist monk, Kuan-hsiu, ca. 895. The stones were set up in the Sheng-yin-sse Temple, Hang-chou.

Evidence has been found indicating that Buddhist and Confucian texts were carved in stone for the purpose of printing books. Examples of this type of publishing, dating from 1200, have survived, and it is definitely known that the use of the rubbing technique to print books was extensive during the Ming dynasty. The best-known examples to have survived are fragments of the series "Prints of the Forest of Mr. Chou," published by Chou Li-ching between 1580 and 1589, which contain treatises on painting and copies of a large number of paintings.

Lastly, the technique of rubbing has been a tool of archaeologists since the Sung period. It was, and still is, particularly well suited to copying tomb carvings (which were probably made with the intent of their being copied at some later date) as well as to serve as monuments to the deceased. The modern archaeologist, in most cases, may forego rubbings in favor of photographs, although the former are more precise and in great demand by most institutions and museums. There is, however, no substitute for the rubbing when studying the surface calligraphy of the ancient bronze vessels of China. Calligraphy was sometimes carved inside the narrow necks or under the handles as well as on the more easily accessible surfaces. Needless to say, photographing calligraphy on the interior surfaces is impossible. The deciphering of these inscriptions was accomplished only through the technique of rubbing.

Once the Chinese artist selected the surface to rub, he would carefully clean and prepare it to receive the paper. The method of rubbing would also have to be decided upon. If the original was of stone or wood and would not be harmed by water, the wet method was used: A multi-layered paper was dampened and laid over the surface. The artist would concoct a mixture to make the paper lie flat; some mixtures were made from plants, while others were composed chiefly of mineral salts. The paper was then brushed or tapped and allowed to dry against the stone or wood surface. Wax was sometimes used to polish the paper before applying the ink, thus insuring a very sharp reproduction.

The ink and tools used varied, but the use of inkstones and dabbers or tampos was common. The inks were composed chiefly of carbon and mineral oils, which were combined with a glue, molded into stick shapes, and dried. In Japan this ink is called *Sumi* and is comparable to our India ink. The stick was ground on a

Chinese rubbing of Kuan Ti (God of War) on horseback. Seventeenth century. (Courtesy The Metropolitan Museum of Art, Gift of Miss Mabel H. Duncan, 1949.)

special dish or stone and mixed with water to produce the ink. The dabbers or tampos were balls of cotton wrapped with layers of oiled cloth and covered with successive layers of still finer materials until the correct size and flexibility were achieved. The ink was applied to the dabber by brush, or a large tampo was saturated with ink and used much the same as a stamp pad. The artist would touch his dabber to this pad and brush over the flat surface of the paper in a more or less circular motion. When dry, the rubbing was removed and could be polished again to give the impression an added luster. It was not uncommon for rubbings to be executed in colors other than black; many were polychromatic.

If the master thought the ground would be harmed by moisture, or if he considered it especially uneven, he would employ the dry method. This procedure was essentially the same as the wet, but with the omission of water. The surface was rubbed with an ink stone especially prepared, with a minimum of glue, to be used in the dry state. The Chinese rubbings of this type are rather gray and soft in appearance.

Regional variations and the artist's own ingenuity make it impossible to list all of the master's materials and tools. The artist would, of course, select inks and papers and construct tools to suit his needs. A dabber used for taking a rubbing of an inscription in a long necked bronze could not be expected to serve to copy a Lo-han tablet.

As in the case of other Chinese art forms and techniques, rubbing spread throughout the Far East. It became common in Japan, although it never approached the popularity or status it had previously enjoyed. During the twentieth century what was thought to be a new type of rubbing began to be practiced in Japan. Called *Gyotaku*, the process involved inking a fish and making an impression of it on paper. A second type of *Gyotaku* was executed exactly as previously explained in the Chinese wet technique. The surface of the fish was cleaned and covered with paper, which was allowed to become damp-dry. It was

then brushed with an inked dabber to produce the rubbing.

Much to the surprise of its would-be originators, a Japanese newspaper uncovered fish prints dating from 1862 in a private museum. According to Dr. Yoshio Hiyama, a Lord Sakai made a prize catch of fish which he ordered printed and rubbed as a record of his triumph. These *Gyotaku* are probably the oldest ever uncovered, although it is possible that the technique was practiced much earlier—perhaps even in China. In 1955, Dr. Hiyama formed the *Gyotaku-no-kai* (Association of Gyotaku), an organization of artists who produce and exhibit fish prints throughout the world. The association has also been responsible for attaining a high degree of perfection in their techniques, which are far superior to those used by Lord Sakai's unidentified artists. Unfortunately, the origin of this most unusual of rubbing techniques is unknown and may forever remain a mystery.

As previously mentioned, the technique of rubbing was very slow to catch on in the West. To this day the wet ink technique is seldom taught or practiced. The dry technique, however, was used in Europe possibly as early as the twelfth century. Unfortunately, no examples have survived to the present day.

The most important European rubbings are those taken from monumental brasses. A monumental brass is an engraved figure, inscription or other design placed to commemorate the deceased. These plates are found throughout central and northwestern Europe. Those in the churches and cathedrals of England are regarded as among the finest in the world. A superb collection dating from 1320 to 1529 is found at Cobham, Kent (commonly called the mecca of brasses).

The brasses were placed in church floors and on walls, but many are almost totally obscured from view by being placed at great heights or under pews. Still others were placed on doors, exterior walls, and in adjoining graveyards.

The earliest brasses were created in the

last quarter of the thirteenth century and the last, in the mid-twentieth century. The popularity of brasses grew with the rise of the middle class. For this reason there are only three existing brasses to royalty, the finest of which is of King Eric Menved and his Queen Ingebord, dated 1319, in Ringstead, Denmark.

Generally speaking, the art of brass engraving reached its highest degree of technical and artistic achievement during the fourteenth century. Brasses of the fifteenth century, for the most part, are composed of small figures and are limited in format. This curious aesthetic confinement was the result of the devastating Black Death, then sweeping Europe. Sixteenth-century works are poorer still and reflect a shift to a more commercial handling of motif. There was a brief renaissance during the Elizabethan Age, but this only served to reduce the engraver's skill to a quaint folk art.

Aside from their obvious historical, artistic, and social significance, monumental brasses are one of the most valuable sources of information on costume and armor. As is true also of armor of the late thirteenth century, fourteenth century, and first half of the fifteenth century, few brasses have survived the ravages of time. Brasses are often the only accurate records of heraldry, design, and military fashion. This one aspect of brasses, deserving of many chapters, is far too extensive to be included here. Let it suffice to say that monumental brasses represent the "types" of the medieval man and records of custom, which remain the most consistently dated art form of the period.

Unlike the grave markers of early New England, which were commissioned after the client had died, the brasses were sometimes engraved during the lifetime of the commemorated. The casting and engraving were done in workshops which usually were a family tradition or guild. To the trained eye, the styles of different artisans or schools of craftsmen are obvious.

Designs were inspired by current philosophies, fine art, and architecture.

Engravers were artists and in many cases worked with stone cutters. Design elements on new brass plates were copied from older examples. This copying was done by the technique of rubbing. The earliest representation of this technique was made by Hendrik van Vliet, in 1656, in his painting of children making rubbings in the interior of the church at Delft (see page 30). Other engravers borrowed freely from drawings, paintings, and other works by practicing artists, among them Lucas Cranach and Albrecht Dürer.

Within the past ten years, the rubbing of monumental brasses has acquired many followers among Europeans and American tourists alike. In England, the Monumental Brass Society, an organization devoted to the study and preservation of brasses, has published many articles on the subject and fosters a great deal of research. The number of people making rubbings has caused many churches to charge fees and some to restrict the making of rubbings to professionals only. While these restrictions do limit the average tourist, there are still many brasses which are easily accessible. It is interesting to note that the thousands of preserved brasses are but a small percent of the original number, which is estimated to have been in the hundreds of thousands.

Changing religious philosophies, the greed of rulers such as Henry VIII and Edward VI, wars, and the use of brasses for secular purposes share the responsibility for the disappearance of many irreplaceable brasses. Stolen brass plates were often sold to engravers who recut new designs. These plates with carving on the reverse side or reworked designs are called "impsests."

Of far greater importance are the brasses destroyed through neglect or even sold by churches. The current interest in monumental brasses, coupled with modern technological advances, should see to the preservation of the remaining brass monuments. It is unfortunate that the New England gravestones cannot be afforded the same privilege.

Six Chinese rubbings of Lo-han (disciples of Buddha). Black ink on paper. Ming dynasty. (Courtesy The Metropolitan Museum of Art, Gift of Miss H. C. Wagner, 1959.)

Chinese rubbing of Lo-han Chota
Panthaka. Black ink on paper. Ming dynasty.

Chinese rubbing of Lo-han Fa-na-p'o-ssu,
Vanavasa. Black ink on paper. Ming dynasty.

Chinese rubbing of unidentified Lo-han.
Black ink on paper. Ming dynasty.

Chinese rubbing of Lo-han Lo-hu-lo or
Rahula. Black ink on paper. Ming dynasty.

Chinese rubbing of Lo-han Yin-kieh-t'e,
Angida. Black ink on paper. Ming dynasty.

Chinese rubbing of Lo-han No-ku-lo or
Nakula. Black ink on paper. Sung dynasty.

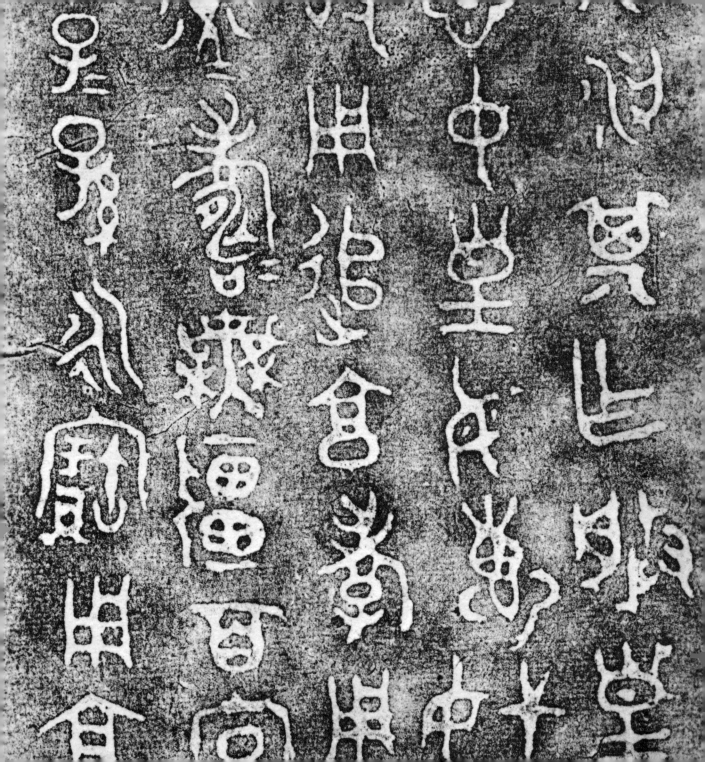

Ink rubbing of Chinese bronze vessel, type *yü*. (Courtesy Smithsonian Institution, Freer Gallery of Art, Washington, D.C.) The first and last characters of the inscription are, as yet, undeciphered. The others repeat the common formula *tso pao tsun i* "...made this precious sacred vessel..."

Opposite Page

Ink rubbing of Chinese bronze vessel, type *kuei*. (Courtesy Smithsonian Institution, Freer Gallery of Art, Washington, D.C.) "I, the Supervisor of Food, Liang Ch'i, have caused to be made this sacred vessel for my deceased father, Hui-chung, and my deceased mother, Hui-yi, in order to reflect my filial piety and in order to make a sacrifice for old age without limit. May you have a hundred sons and a thousand grandsons. May the sons' sons and the grandsons' grandsons treasure it in order to make offerings."

Chinese ink rubbing from stone reliefs at a
family shrine, We-shih-tz'u, in Shan-tung
Province, China. Late Han dynasty, ca.
A.D. 147. (Courtesy the Cleveland Museum
of Art, Gift of Yamanaka and Company,
New York.)

Twentieth-century Chinese ink rubbing of a
leather stencil depicting T'ai Tsung horse.
Ink on paper. (Courtesy The Metropolitan
Museum of Art, Seymour Fund, 1954.)

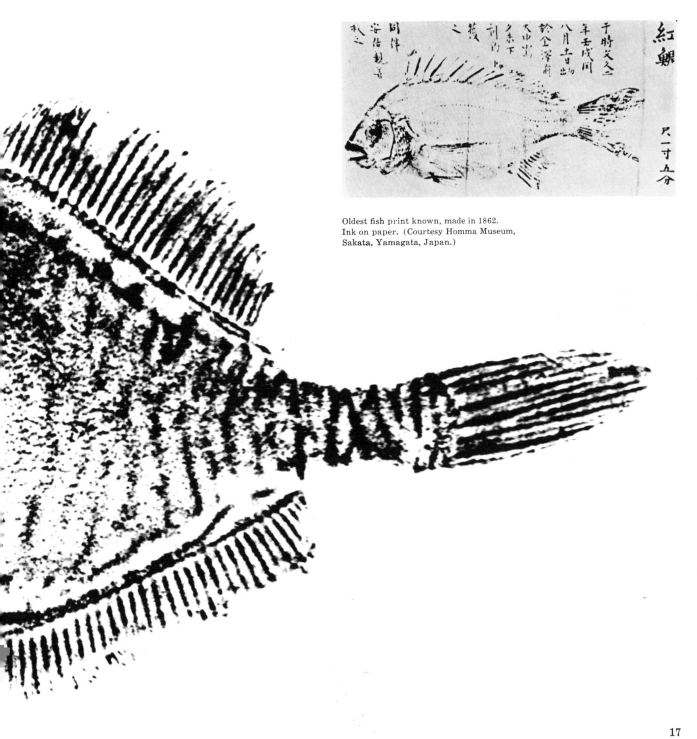

紅鯛

尺一寸五分

于時文久二
年壬戌閏
八月十吉
於金澤村
大山出
久米下
刻印
同伴
安倍靱負
秋之

Oldest fish print known, made in 1862.
Ink on paper. (Courtesy Homma Museum,
Sakata, Yamagata, Japan.)

Rubbing of a zebra fish by Dr. Yoshio
Hiyama. Ink on paper. (Courtesy Dr.
Yoshio Hiyama from *Gyotaku.*)

Opposite Page

Rubbing of a relief depicting a Hindu
legend. Ink on paper. (Courtesy Mr. and
Mrs. Michael De Rosa, Pine Brook,
New Jersey.)

Above. Rubbing of Thai musicians from the marble relief on the walls of the Temple of the Reclining Buddha, Bangkok, Thailand. Rubbing by Visit Srinava. Dry ink stick on paper. (Courtesy the artist.)

Below. Rubbing of ceremonial elephants from the marble relief on the walls of the Temple of the Reclining Buddha, Bangkok, Thailand. Rubbing by Visit Srinava. Dry ink stick on paper. (Courtesy the artist.)

Opposite Page

Rubbing of Thai dancers. Ink on paper. (Courtesy Mr. and Mrs. Michael De Rosa, Pine Brook, New Jersey.)

Rubbing of fish and reptile forms from Angkor Wat, Cambodia. Ink on paper. (Courtesy the Weyhe Gallery, New York.)

Rubbing of Surya, on his throne drawn by horses. Ink on paper. (Courtesy the Weyhe Gallery, New York.)

Rubbing of an inscription from Angkor Wat, Cambodia. Ink on paper. (Courtesy the Weyhe Gallery, New York.)

Rubbing depicts a scene from the Churning of the
Sea of Milk from Angkor Wat, Cambodia. Ink
on paper. (Courtesy the Weyhe Gallery, New York.)

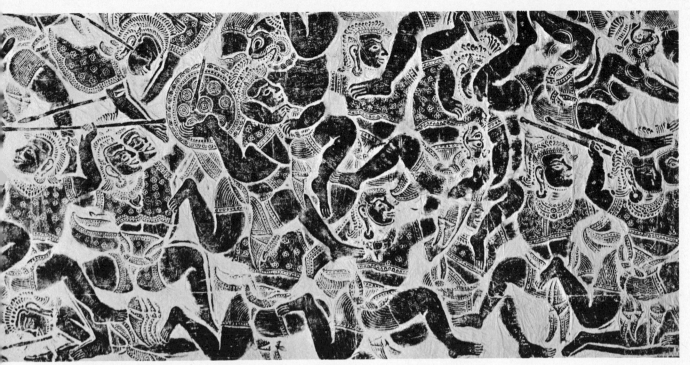

Above and below. Rubbings from Angkor Wat,
Cambodia. Ink on paper. (Courtesy the Weyhe
Gallery, New York.)

Opposite Page
Rubbing from Angkor Wat, Cambodia. Ink on paper.
(Courtesy the Weyhe Gallery, New York.)

Rubbing by Robert S. Lindsley of a relief showing a maternity figure from the prehistoric site at San Augustine, Columbia. Ink on paper. (Courtesy Eugene Fuller Memorial Collection, Seattle Art Museum, Seattle, Washington.)

Rubbing by Robert S. Lindsley of a Pre-Columbian sculptured tablet in The Palace, Palenque, State of Chiapas, Mexico. Original carved before the middle of the eighth century. Ink on paper. (Courtesy Eugene Fuller Memorial Collection, Seattle Art Museum, Seattle, Washington.)

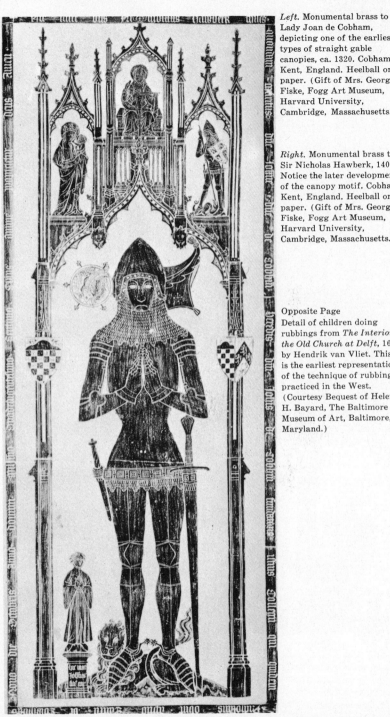

Left. Monumental brass to Lady Joan de Cobham, depicting one of the earliest types of straight gable canopies, ca. 1320. Cobham, Kent, England. Heelball on paper. (Gift of Mrs. George Fiske, Fogg Art Museum, Harvard University, Cambridge, Massachusetts.)

Right. Monumental brass to Sir Nicholas Hawberk, 1407. Notice the later development of the canopy motif. Cobham, Kent, England. Heelball on paper. (Gift of Mrs. George Fiske, Fogg Art Museum, Harvard University, Cambridge, Massachusetts.)

Opposite Page
Detail of children doing rubbings from *The Interior of the Old Church at Delft*, 1656, by Hendrik van Vliet. This is the earliest representation of the technique of rubbing as practiced in the West. (Courtesy Bequest of Helen H. Bayard, The Baltimore Museum of Art, Baltimore, Maryland.)

Monumental brass to John Gray, ca. 1392.
Oxon, England. Heelball on paper. (Courtesy
The British Museum, London.)

Monumental brass to Elizabeth, wife of
Sir Roger de Northwood, 1335. Kent,
England. Heelball on paper. (Courtesy The
British Museum, London.)

Monumental brass to Sir John Harpedon,
died in 1436. One of the best brasses of the
period. Westminster Abbey, London.
Rubbing by Michael Black, Oxford, England.
Heelball on paper. (Courtesy the artist.)

Monumental brass to Sir Roger de
Trumpington, died 1287, the only "crusader"
known to have gone to the Crusades.
Trumpington, Cambridge, England. Rubbing
by Michael Black, Oxford, England.
Heelball on paper. (Courtesy the artist.)

Monumental brass to Eleanor of Bohin,
Duchess of Gloucester. Notice the
widow's wimple and veil. Westminster
Abbey, London, 1399. Rubbing by
Michael Black, Oxford, England.
Heelball on paper. (Courtesy the artist.)

Monumental brass to Sir Symon
Felbrygge, K.G. The inscribed
garter signifies his membership in the
Most Noble Order of the Garter. Rubbing
by Michael Black, Oxford, England. Heelball on
paper. (Courtesy the artist.)

Here resteth the bodies of Simon Parret Gentilman: master of arte: late fellowe of Magdalen Colledg: and twise procter of the vniuersitie of Oxford: and Eliza-beth his wife: Doughter of Edward Loue of Aenohe: in the coonte of North-hampton Elqnuer: Which Simon Departed this worlde the 24: day of Septe in the yere of owre lorde God M CCCC 84: and in the yere of his age 71: and Elizabeth Departed in childbed the xxiiii day of December in the yere of owre lorde God M CCCC lxxii: and in the yere of her age xliij

Monumental brass to Simon Parret, Master of Arts,
Fellow of Magdalen College, died 1584, aged 71.
Rubbing by Michael Black, Oxford, England.
Heelball on paper. (Courtesy the artist.)

Opposite Page
Monumental brass to Richard Notfeld. There are
quite a few skeletons like this, some complete with
worms. Near Cambridge. Rubbing by Michael
Black, Oxford, England. White heelball on black
paper. (Courtesy the artist.)

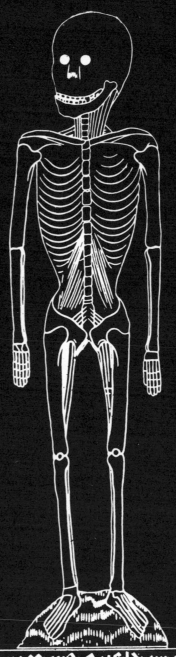

Orate p anima Ricardi Rotcerld qui obut penult[i]o
die m[en]s[is] marcii A[nn]o d[omi]ni m[illesi]mo cccc xlvj

Monumental brass to Sir
Reginald Malyns and wives,
ca. 1385. Chinnor, Oxon,
England. Heelball on paper.
(Courtesy The British
Museum, London.)

Monumental brass to Nicholas and Dorothy Wadham, 1618. By the seventeenth century armor was ornamental rather than functional. This brass is perhaps the finest example of this style. Ilminster, Somerset, England. Rubbing by Michael Black, Oxford, England. Heelball on paper. (Courtesy the artist.)

Icon rubbing depicting
St. George on Horseback,
1676. (Collection the Museum
of Applied Art, Belgrade.)

Icon rubbing depicting
St. Nicholas, first half of the
seventeenth century.
(Collection the Museum of
Applied Art, Belgrade.)

MORY OF THE MEN FROM OSS
RCLIFF AND SCARBOROUGH

2.
Subject Matter and Design

In its purest sense, the technique of rubbing is the lifting of a design from a pre-formed or carved surface. Usually the artist is not involved with the production of the "original" surface. For many, the aspect of originality has been a deterent to their investigation of this ancient technique. It is strange to see these same people sign their names to a landscape, play tic-tac-toe on a Laliberté game banner or buy a soup can by Andy Warhol, for the "originality" of these, too, could be questioned.

The originality of a rubbing lies in the selection of the surface and in the choice and handling of the media. Needless to say, this is somewhat limited when the sole aim of the artist is to copy a surface to preserve it for posterity. The contemporary artist working in collage and related techniques, however, experiences no such limitation. In the selection of the surface to rub, the artist isolates a tactile or visual form from the hundreds of thousands which daily pass in disarray before him. He also effects a kind of

transformation of that design by making a two-dimensional graphic representation of a three-dimensional texture, shape, or carving. Through the simple technique of rubbing he converts texture to pattern, yielding a bold, minutely detailed image.

There is no problem finding objects or surfaces to rub. The more academic artist is apt to choose gravestones, brasses, architectural reliefs, commemorative medals, incised designs or pictures.

We have been witnesses to junk art, assemblage, disassemblage, and the work of the Pop artists. Any product or by-product of our culture is suitable material for a work of art and, consequently, useful for making rubbings. There is the added advantage that the article may be used in spite of value or size, since it is not harmed or moved during the process. Manhole covers, signs, fencing, walls, pavements, toys, parts of any machine or tool, from a refrigerator to a computer, can be successfully used for a rubbing.

The artist has long relied on nature for inspiration and this source should not be

overlooked when searching for material for rubbings. Bark, stones, bones, leaves, flowers, fish, and seed pods will make surprising patterns.

Once the combining of elements on a picture plane is begun, the personality of the artist begins to become evident. He is imposing an artistic order on the things he is rubbing. While anyone can make a rubbing, the more inventive a person is in his selection of surfaces, and the more sensitive to design, the more successful the work.

While some prefer to start with a preconceived idea, this is by no means a prerequisite for a successful rubbing. It is possibly best to begin simply and allow the idea to develop as the work is completed.

The subject matter and designs illustrated in this chapter have been drawn from many sources. The challenge to the student and artist alike is to isolate those textures and forms to which they respond and combine them in a graphic organization.

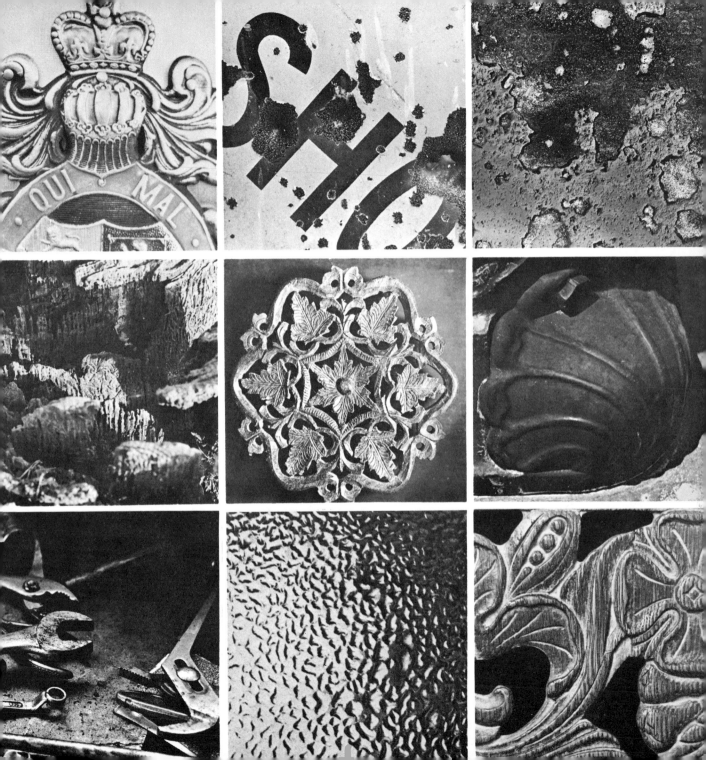

3.
Materials and Procedures

MATERIALS

Unless otherwise indicated, all
materials required for the five
techniques discussed in this chapter
can be obtained from the address below.
A free catalog of rubbing supplies
is available upon request.

New York Central Supply
62 Third Avenue
New York, N.Y. 10003

Paper for making proofs:
  newsprint
  wrapping paper
Paper for making final rubbing:
  3M rubbing fabric
  detail paper
  charcoal paper
  bristol board, single ply, plate finish
  speed-ball printing paper
  rice papers: masa, boyu, hosho,
        troya, torinoko
Scissors
Masking tape to hold the paper in place
Rubbing media:
  primary crayons
  lumber crayons
  graphite sticks
  charcoal
  etcher's ground
  tailor's chalk
  lithographic rubbing ink (hard)
  heelball (Phillips & Page, Ltd., 50
        Kensington Church St., London
        W.8., England)
Stiff brush for cleaning the surface
        (hardware store)
Toothbrush for cleaning small details
        (drugstore)
Putty knife for scraping hard-to-remove
        foreign matter
Paper towels or pre-moistened wiping
        tissue for keeping hands clean
        (supermarket)

Cylinder to hold roll of large paper
Folder of portfolio to hold paper
Small paper bag for refuse
Spray fixative
Kneeling pad or carpet sample
        (garden supply or carpet store)
Pencil for labeling

PROCEDURE

The explanations of the dry technique and
the techniques that follow are illustrated
by using the surfaces of tombstones for
examples, but are by no means limited to
them. Readers wishing to take rubbings
of other surfaces should follow the same
procedures, whether the surface is a
manhole cover or a coin, allowing for the
obvious differences in size, location, and
texture.

Selecting the surface to rub is very
important. With gravestones, only un-
damaged surfaces bearing finely cut
designs should be rubbed. Once the stone
is decided upon, all foreign material
should be removed with the brushes or
putty knife.

Lichen may present a minor problem,
since scraping is the only method of
removal. Its elimination is essential for
obtaining a fine rubbing. If allowed to
remain, the lichen will produce dark,
unattractive blotches on the rubbing.
When rubbing the entire stone, it may be
necessary to cut the grass growing at its
base. It, too, will appear in the print if
allowed to remain.

After the surface is clean, the proof
paper (newsprint is best for this) is cut
to size and taped in place so that at least
a one-inch border remains. (For the
sake of brevity, this is not illustrated.
Follow the pictures illustrating taping
the final paper.) The first piece of masking tape should be put in the center of the
top edge, the second opposite on the bot-

tom, the third on the center of the right
side, the fourth opposite on the left. If
additional pieces of tape are required
they should be placed between the first
four pieces and directly opposite each
other. The paper should be smoothed out
from the center with the free hand before
adhering each piece.

Almost any dry medium will produce
a rubbing, but wax crayon is most
commonly used. Primary crayons are
particularly good because they are
slightly thicker and have one flat side (to
keep them from rolling off children's
desks). The paper wrapper should be
removed to allow the smooth surface to be
fully utilized. Connoisseurs prefer to use
a heelball stick or cake. Heelball is a
mixture of beeswax, tallow, and lamp
black, which is used by cobblers as a
polish. A special permanent heelball is
made exclusively for rubbing. Prepared
at the request of the Monumental Brass
Society, this type must be imported from
England.

When making the proof, the entire
surface of the paper is rubbed briskly
with the broad flat side of the medium.
Wherever the paper comes into contact
with the raised surface beneath it, the
rubbing medium will register. Sunken
areas remain white. The purpose of this
preliminary rubbing is to point up any
flaws or cracks in the surface and to
indicate large negative (incised) areas
which must be avoided. Frequently, surfaces that yield poor or weak proofs are
bypassed, saving the good paper for more
suitable examples.

If the proof suggests that the surface
is suitable, the good paper is taped in
place as previously explained, but as
close to the edges as possible. The paper
must, however, be held securely in place
because shifting will cause blurring of the

1. The first step in making a rubbing by any of the techniques is to clean the surface thoroughly. Very dirty surfaces may have to be washed or scraped.

2. Adhering the paper to the surface for the dry technique. Pieces of masking tape are placed opposite each other. The paper should lie perfectly flat. Wrinkles can be removed by peeling the tape off the surface and smoothing from the center out.

image. Almost any type of strong, thin, linen-base paper can be used for the final rubbing. Large sheets of detail paper, used by architects, are good as are other types of artist's paper.

Unlike the proof, the final rubbing is begun by working delicately from the center out. The large negative areas, cracks, and depressions are avoided by constantly referring to the proof and feeling for them with the fingers of the free hand.

The novice is sometimes aided by making a "hand" rubbing before attempting the final print. This is done by rubbing the entire surface of the paper with the hands to expose the raised areas. (A word of caution: Some of the crayon

from previous rubbing will have inevitably soiled the hands, so it is always wise to clean them before beginning.) Once most of the design is visible, the crayon is applied. After the entire design is established lightly, the procedure is repeated. This time a moderate pressure is placed on the marking implement and the rubbing is completed, working carefully from the edges in. Before the paper is removed, the image should be checked at a distance for evenness of color. Sometimes, because of the vigor with which the rubbing is begun, some portions will be much darker than others. After the weaker areas are corrected, the tape can be peeled off the paper, freeing the print. The tape should never be peeled off the

stone toward the paper.

After returning home with a selection of rubbings, you may notice that some imperfections did not register at all. While coloring in these white spots may prove satisfactory, it may be necessary to "draw" in the missing textures. Another method of correction is to place a piece of stone which has a texture close to that of the original under the portion of the paper where the white spot appears and rub carefully. Depending on the medium used, stray marks can prove next to impossible to remove. Crayon and heelball are the most difficult to erase. Scraping with a razor blade and painting with an opaque retouching white are possible methods of making minor corrections.

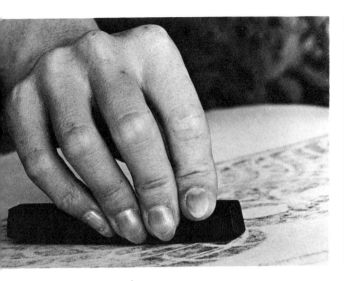

3. The stick of heelball is grasped firmly and carefully applied to the paper's surface.

4. When the stick is worked delicately from the center out, the raised areas underneath are revealed.

5. After the entire design is established, the surface is again rubbed, this time pressing heavily.

6. When complete, the rubbing is removed by carefully peeling the masking tape off the paper.

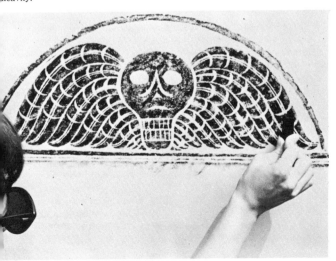

WET TECHNIQUE

MATERIALS

Proof paper:
    brown wrapping
    bristol board, two-ply, plate finish
Final paper:
    rice papers: haruki, natsume,
        kinwashi, moriki
Scissors
Chamois
Dabbers of various sizes
Ink: India ink, printer's ink or sumi;
    or watercolor
Stiff brush
Toothbrush
Putty knife
Paper towels or tissue
Squeeze bottle or atomizer of water
Methylcellulose (powder or tablets)
Elephant ear sponge for applying
    methylcellulose
Clothing brush
Cylinder or portfolio
Archer's wax
Kneeling pad or carpet sample
Pencil for labeling

PROCEDURE

The wet technique of rubbing is considerably harder to master than the dry method. Patience and practice are prerequisites to producing satisfactory ink rubbings.

Deeply carved, uneven, and rounded stones are best suited for reproduction with this method. The stone is cleaned as previously explained and the paper measured and cut. Japanese papers are best for ink rubbings because of their fiber content and strength when wet.

While the paper is held in place on top of the design, it is wet with a mixture of methylcellulose and water. Methylcellulose is a chemical used to promote normal peristalsis (contraction) and is available at any drugstore in tablet form (see Technical Notes). It can be applied to the paper with the fingers or with a small elephant ear sponge. Since the methylcellulose is a mild glue, tape is not necessary to hold the paper in place. All air bubbles should be eliminated by working gently from the center out with the hands, and the paper should cling flatly to the entire surface of the design. Some prefer to apply the ink while the paper is damp, while others, including the author, allow the entire surface to dry thoroughly.

The next step is optional and may be used only with inks and colors that contain little or no water. The dry paper is brushed with beeswax—the type made for archer's bow strings is acceptable. A soft hair or soft bristle clothing brush is ideal for applying the wax. The paper must be brushed in all directions, delicately at first, then increasing in vigor until the paper's surface is polished. This coat of wax will insure a sharp image and will stop the color from penetrating the paper.

The ink is applied with a dabber or tampo. This is a ball of sponge covered with several layers of cotton cloth surrounded by a piece of chamois. The ends of the material are tied off with thin wire, string or rubber bands. Other dabbers can be covered with fine silk, linen, cotton or some synthetic fibers. It is a good idea to have several sizes of dabbers on hand because it may be necessary to switch during the same rubbing.

There are several ways of inking the tampo. The least acceptable is to pour the ink directly onto the pad. Aside from the running and obvious mess, dabbers inked this way will mark unevenly. An alternate method is to fill a small shallow dish with ink and dip the tampo, squeezing off the excess ink on the outside lip of the dish. The best method is to make a large dabber and saturate it with the ink. This is then used as a stamp pad. The tampo used for the rubbing is touched to this pad as needed.

As soon as the dabber is inked, the rubbing can be begun. The excess ink is removed by touching a piece of scrap paper with the dabber before attempting to copy the design. This must be done after each inking. The dabber must never rest on the good paper, but, rather, be brushed horizontally across its surface. This requires a good deal of practice, and the novice should not be discouraged if his first "wet" rubbing is not up to his expectations. With experience comes the privilege of darkening certain areas while keeping others gray or clean. When a polychromatic rubbing is to be made, the light colors are applied first followed by the darker hues.

The finished rubbing is allowed to dry and is then peeled off the surface with a constant, even pull. Because of the methylcellulose, the paper will roll, making transporting easy.

When preparing the rubbing for display, the curl can be eliminated by pressing the rubbing under a flat board or by mounting it with photographic dry mount tissue.

1. After the stone is cleaned, the paper (Japanese fiber) is cut to size and stuck to the surface with a mixture of methylcellulose.

2. While the paper is still wet, all air bubbles are removed. The paper is allowed to dry thoroughly.

3. The surface of the paper is polished with beeswax and a soft brush. This will insure a sharp image.

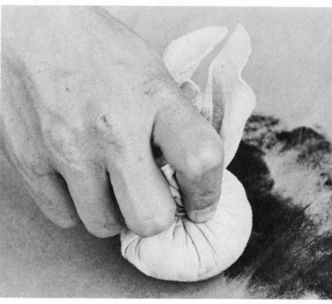

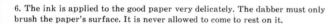

4. A large dabber is saturated with ink. Ink from this large pad is transferred onto a smaller dabber which will be used to make the rubbing.

5. Excess ink is removed by touching the small dabber to a piece of scrap paper. This procedure is repeated after each inking.

6. The ink is applied to the good paper very delicately. The dabber must only brush the paper's surface. It is never allowed to come to rest on it.

7. The ink is allowed to dry thoroughly before the paper is removed. This is done by firmly gripping the paper with both hands and pulling from the bottom up.

DABBING TECHNIQUE

MATERIALS

Paper: deberasu rice paper, tissue
Scrap paper to test dabber
Plastic squeeze bottle or atomizer of water
    for washing stone, hands, and
    shrinking paper
Scissors
Masking tape to hold paper in place
Small wood board on which to mix oil
    and graphite
Linseed oil
Powdered graphite
Chamois covered dabber or tampo to apply
    graphite and oil mixture
Spray fixative
Pencil for labeling

PROCEDURE

In the dabbing technique the paper is the same as that used for the carbon technique. The paper is also mounted on the stone in the same manner. On a small board, powdered graphite is mixed with a few drops of linseed oil to produce a paste. The tampo is rubbed in the paste. After the excess has been scraped off and the dabber tested on the scrap paper, the surface is rubbed as in the wet technique. This rubbing technique is similar to the carbon technique in that it tends to copy the smallest details of the surface. It, too, must be lightly sprayed with fixative to prevent smearing.

55

CARBON TECHNIQUE

MATERIALS

Paper:
  carbon (stationery store)
  newsprint for covering carbon paper
  graphite paper
  good rice paper: deberasu, chiri,
    yamato (light), sekishu
    (natural and white)
Plastic squeeze bottle or atomizer of water
  (for washing stone, hands, or
  shrinking paper)
Scissors
Masking tape to hold the paper in place
Burin, bamboo rice paddle or rubber shoe
  heel to rub with

Spray fixative
Pencil for labeling

PROCEDURE

This method is particularly well suited to copying smooth stones and very delicately incised designs. The area to be copied is covered with the good paper and taped. Airmail weight paper or Japanese print paper is best. The paper is then sprayed with water, which will cause it to sag. The tape is removed from the stone and re-stuck, pulling the paper still tighter. As the water evaporates, the paper will shrink and be stretched very tight. It is advantageous to add extra pieces of tape before the paper is dry. A large

sheet of newsprint is taped to the back of the top of the stone and allowed to hang over the front side covering the stretched paper. The carbon paper is placed, carbon side facing the design, between the two sheets. While it is held in place with one hand, it is rubbed with the other. Almost any hard, flat object can be used to rub. It is, however, possible to rip through one or all of the papers. Therefore, a piece of hard rubber, shoe heel, printing burin or bamboo rice paddle is most commonly used. The carbon rubbing will never be as dark as the other dry media rubbings, but it records more detail than any previously discussed. The finished rubbing is sprayed with a charcoal fixative to prevent smearing.

Very thin tissue paper is taped to the stone as before. It is then sprayed with water, which will cause it to sag. Each piece of tape is removed in turn from the stone and replaced, pulling the paper still tighter. Upon drying, the

paper will shrink and be drawn tightly across the surface. Paper prepared by this process is suitable for making rubbings by the carbon or dabbing technique.

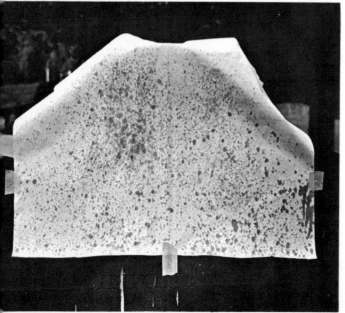

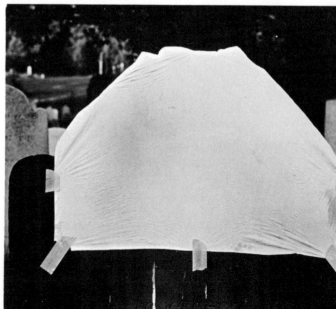

56

Example of a rubbing made with the carbon technique.

FOIL TECHNIQUE

MATERIALS

Copper or aluminum tooling
Sharpened dowels of different sizes to
    rub foil
Steel wool, fine and medium, to polish foil
    (hardware store)
Masking tape to hold foil in place
Sponge to rub foil (hardware store)
Plaster of paris for backing foil rubbing
Rubber mixing bowl to mix plaster
Hot plate or propane gas torch to heat liver
    of sulphur solution (hardware store)
Liver of sulphur (hardware store)
½-inch brush to apply liver of sulphur
    solution
Clear plastic spray to prevent oxidation
    of copper
Epoxy cement to mount light rubbings
Wooden plaque for mounting rubbing
    (lumber supply)
Wood stain or varnish to finish plaque
    (hardware store)
¼-inch screw eyes to hang plaque
    (hardware store)
Picture wire to hang picture
Sparex to remove oxidation from
    copper foil
⅛-inch, round-head brass wood screws
    to mount rubbing
Screwdriver (hardware store)
Drill and bit (hardware store)

PROCEDURE

Strictly speaking, the foil technique of
rubbing is a craft activity called "tooling."
The metal sheets are usually pressed
into concave plastic molds yielding a low
relief picture.

This method is, however, equally well
suited to copying textures and low
relief sculptures such as tombstones.

The stone is cleaned and the tooling
foil cut to size and taped in place. It is
then rubbed with the hands and, next,
with a dry sponge to reveal the general
outline of the underlying design. As
before, the rubbing is done from the center
out. Once the design is clearly established,
the design is rubbed with the ends of
dowels which have been rounded to dull
points. Many such dowels of varying sizes
are necessary for any one rubbing. Each
part of the design must be rubbed in
order, working from the center out. In this
way the extra material is pushed toward
the outer edges of the stone and eventually
folded over. The finished rubbing is
polished with fine steel wool and removed.
The bottom edge is folded back and
joined to the top curve so as to form a
type of shallow pan or mold. The corners
are likewise folded and taped. Any holes,
caused by too much pressure on the
dowels, are now sealed from the back with
masking tape. All holes and joints must
be sealed before mixing the plaster.

A rubber bowl (a discarded half of a
kick ball is excellent for this) is half
filled with water. Plaster of paris is sifted
into the bowl until the water surface is
just over that of the plaster. After mixing
by hand to a smooth consistency, the
plaster is poured into the mold. Although
it will harden within minutes, the mold
should be allowed to dry overnight before
continuing the process (see Technical
Notes).

When the plaster is dry, the surplus
edges of foil are folded over against the
back of the mold to prevent the plaster
core from falling out. The face is first
cleaned with a soft cloth dampened with a
Sparex solution and then polished with
fine steel wool. If this surface is desirable
it should be sprayed with clear plastic
or varnish.

Those wishing to age the surface to
create a rich patina can accomplish this
by painting the face with a mixture of
hot liver of sulphur. Liver of sulphur can
be purchased in liquid form or as dry
chunks. The heating or dissolving should
be done in a well ventilated place—
preferably outside, since the fumes are
extremely toxic (see Technical Notes).
The mixture will turn the surface of the
copper black. This scale can be partially
removed by washing with water. The
remaining oxides, when polished with steel
wool, will appear quite lustrous. This
procedure may be repeated as many times
as necessary until the desired surface is
achieved. The piece is finished by buffing
with jeweler's rouge.

The foil rubbing can be hung as is by
gluing screw eyes into the back. Larger
rubbings, because of their weight, usually
require mounting on a wood plaque. This
is done by nailing wood strips, attaching
"L" braces, or drilling holes through the
plaster and attaching it to the plaque with
brass round-head wood screws.

It is conceivable that stones could be
damaged by an abuse of this method; the
reader is asked to exercise his good
judgment in the practice of making foil
rubbings.

1. The foil is measured and cut to a size slightly larger than the surface to be rubbed.

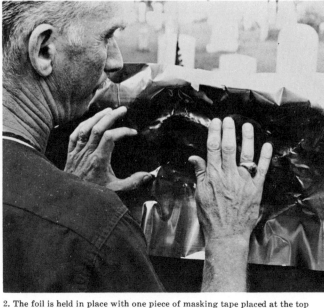

2. The foil is held in place with one piece of masking tape placed at the top center edge of the foil. Working from the center out, the copper foil is pressed against the stone and into the large concavities, first with the hands and then with a dry sponge. While this will tend to hold the foil in place, additional pieces of tape are stuck wherever needed.

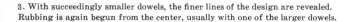

3. With succeedingly smaller dowels, the finer lines of the design are revealed. Rubbing is again begun from the center, usually with one of the larger dowels.

4. Note the double-ended dowel sharpened to blunt and pointed ends.

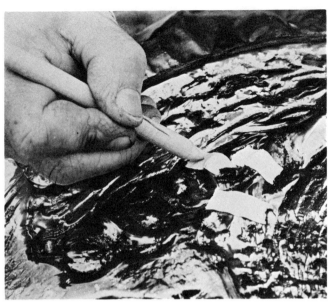

5. Holes in the foil may be caused by too much pressure on the dowel or by deep concavities in the surface of the stone. These can be patched successfully with masking tape applied to the back.

6. Edges of the foil are folded back to form a sort of mold which will contain the plaster of paris. The corners are securely taped to prevent the plaster from leaking out.

7. The plaster is allowed to harden for at least twenty-four hours. The foil surface is polished with steel wool and washed thoroughly with Sparex, which will remove all oxides and tarnish. The Sparex in turn is washed off with clear water.

8. Liver of sulphur is dissolved in a can of water heated with a propane gas torch (or over a hot plate).

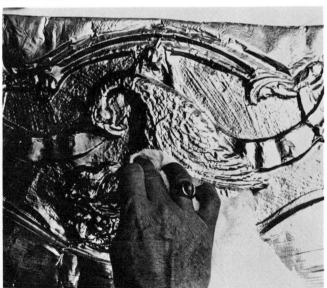

9. The warm mixture of liver of sulphur is painted over the foil rubbing.

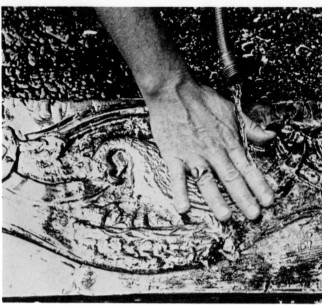

10. After a few minutes, the surface is again washed with water. This process is repeated until the desired surface quality is achieved.

11. The surface is finished by buffing with fine steel wool and wiping with a soft cloth.

12. The finished surface can be enhanced further by spraying with a fixative or varnish.

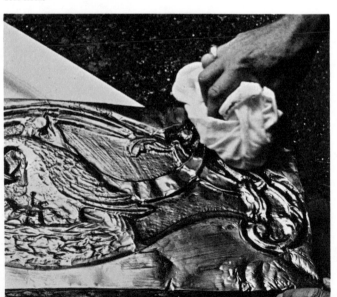

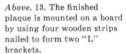

Above. 13. The finished plaque is mounted on a board by using four wooden strips nailed to form two "L" brackets.

This plaque was glued to a wooden plank.

4.
Early New England Gravestones

The most popular rubbings made in the United States, as in England, are taken from funerary monuments. The lure of the Puritan tombstones erected from 1650 to 1815 is hard to ignore. Most striking are the carvings of skulls combined with macabre lines of poetry:

As you are now,
So once was I;
As I am now,
So you must be.
So prepare for death
and follow me.

The markers were made chiefly of slate, white marble, syenite, redstone, quartzite, schist, greenstone (beech-bowlder) or freestone which came from New England quarries. The stonecutters, at least in the mid-seventeenth century, and in rural areas, probably plied several other crafts, carving an occasional stone when the need arose. One carver, Joshua Hempstead, was a carpenter, farmer, judge of probate, land broker, and mariner. As the population grew, so did the need for stone carvers; during the eighteenth century there were well over fifty carvers in the Boston region alone. Some became quite well known, set up workshops, and passed the craft down from father to son for generations. The names of some carvers appear on the stones themselves, while others, because of style or technique, are attributed to individual carvers.

Much of the uncertainty about all aspects of New England gravestone carving, notably the meaning and origin of the low relief carvings, has just recently been removed, largely through the efforts of Dr. Allan I. Ludwig of Dickinson College. As a result of his studies, and those of the late Harriette Merrifield Forbes, many theories concerning the ancient markers are now universally accepted.

The purpose of the Puritan tombstone was to instruct the congregation as well as to remember and honor the departed soul. The largely illiterate population was taught through the carved symbols and forewarned of man's confrontation with death. We can only speculate as to how much the family of the deceased, their religious leaders or the severity of the Puritan faith influenced individual stone carvers. It is evident that changing religious attitudes during the eighteenth century were responsible for the portrayal of less formidable figures and designs and ultimately their complete replacement by the neoclassical style by 1815.

To the twentieth-century eye, the carving on the slabs ranges from primitive to sophisticated, naturalistic to abstract. Recalling the textbook account of the Puritan's colonization, religion, and customs, it is not difficult to understand the grinning skull flanked by wings as death's triumph. We also have little trouble understanding the frightening allegory of Father Time accompanying the Grim Reaper as he snuffs out the flame of life. Less easy to understand, however, are the carvings of soul effigies and angels, which are often impossible to tell apart. They are equipped with wings to aid them in their flight to heaven and may wear the crown of righteousness. Still other souls may be pictured as glorified or

trumpeting, announcing the resurrection. Coffins, tombs, cinerary urns, shovels, picks and bones symbolize the death of the flesh and are often juxtaposed with flowers, trees, and other symbols of life. The overall shape of the stones, borrowed from architecture, suggests the doorway to heaven or the passageway to the unknown. The meanings of several symbols are not completely understood. Among them, the geometric rosettes, swirls and discs, which replaced the effigies on some stones. While many of the design motifs dealt with man and his relation to the Almighty, the historical significance of the origin of the designs and the unique place in our American heritage occupied by this art form cannot be overlooked.

The practice of erecting a carved headstone, and several of the designs, came to this country from England with the Puritans. Individual motifs, however, are found throughout the world. A geometric rosette appears on a Roman stone in England; peacocks were long used by the Byzantines; an almost exact copy of a medieval reclining skeleton mosaic appears on a stone in Massachusetts; and countless other carvings seem to be copies of engravings and woodcuts in books. The constant discovery of such similarities raises a number of interesting questions about the authenticity or originality of the stonecutter's designs.

The tombstone was the first sculpture created by colonial settlers. For the young student and scholar, visiting colonial graveyards makes the history of our nation come alive, both from the standpoint of the art form and the events to which the stones bear witness. The epitaphs in the Boston vicinity tell of heroes, battles, victories, and defeats of the Revolutionary era. Other monuments bear the unmistakable scars of vicious battles. One such stone in Ossining, New York, displays a hole which was made by a cannon ball fired from a British warship as she sailed up the Hudson River.

It might be noted here that although the stone cutter's art was practiced principally in the New England states it was not confined to that region. Excellent carvings can be found in New York State. Trinity Church in Lower Manhattan and Flatbush Reformed Church in Brooklyn possess bucolic graveyards as do Staten Island and the surrounding southern counties.

Most cemeteries are open to the public and rubbings can easily be taken. When a graveyard adjoins a rectory or is locked, it is courteous to request permission to enter to make rubbings. Often the pastor or custodian will gladly oblige and conduct the visitor on a guided tour. It is important to remember to take all paper, tape, etc., when leaving and also to exercise great care so that the stones rubbed do not bear traces of the media used.

Even in many bustling cities the old burying ground has maintained its unique quality of profound peace, soliloquy, and eternal repose. But the visitor is often dismayed at the rate at which the ancient markers are giving way to the natural ravages of time and weather. Scores of stones are split every winter when moisture in minute cracks expands upon freezing. Epitaphs cut in softer stones are worn smooth and bear soft shadows of their once poignant messages. Of greater concern are the large numbers of superb sculptures defaced by vandals. The author has found countless examples of stones that have withstood a century and a half of nature's fury only to succumb to the unwarranted destruction of man. Historical societies and caretakers have made some feeble attempts at restoring and preserving the disintegrating monuments, but there is little that can be done to restore an effigy's head shattered by a well-aimed bullet.

Annually hundreds of stones succumb to the ravages of time, nature, and man.

The Daniel Chapman stone, 1741, Westport, Connecticut, was permanently defaced when someone, attempting to copy the design, inked the carving with an oil-base printer's ink.

Gravestone Rubbings by the Author

The rubbings in this section will give the reader a brief survey of the technique as it can be applied to recording early New England tombstones. While many examples are from Boston and other New England colonial centers, others were taken from stones in New York State. Almost all of the rubbings were made with heelball or crayon on 3M rubbing fabric.

To the Memory of
M.r LEMUEL CAMP
who on the 31.st Day of Jan.ry A.D.1784
in the 83.d Year of his Age.
In obedience to Natures Law, with
Meeknefs & Chriftian Fortitude
refigned his Life to the
Almighty giver
and quietly fell
afleep.
This Monument is infcrib'd

The Marble monument muft yeild to Time

Deacon Mathias Rice, 1764, Northboro, Massachusetts.

Fugit

DEPOSITED
Beneath this Stone the Mortal Part
of Mrs. SUSANNA JAYNE, the amiable Wife of
Mr. PETER JAYNE, who lived Beloved
and Died Universally Lamented on
August 8th 1776 in the 45th
Year of her Age.

Here lies Interd the Remains of the
Respectable ELISHA LYON Eldest Son of
Cap: NEHEMIAH LYON & MEHETABLE his
wife. He died Oct. 15th 1767 in the 24th
Year of His Age. His Death is mournfully
memorable on account of the manner and
occasion. For as He was Decently going
thro the military manual Exercise. in the
Company under Comand of Capt ELISHA
CHILD. Sd Capt Giving the words of
Command He was Wounded by the
discharge of Fire arms. used by one of
the Company Sd arms having been
Loaded Intirely unknown to him;
the wound was Instantaneous DEATH

Example of a rubbing
produced with the
carbon technique.

In Memory of
Lovice Daughter
of Mr. Silas &
Mrs. Eunice Dunten
who died
Feb. 10. 1786
In Her 4 year
A Law Eternal
does decree:
That all things born

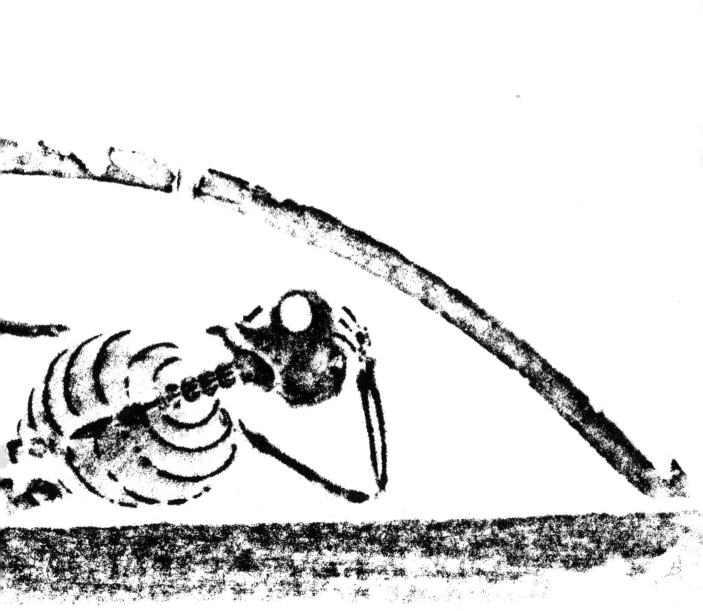

Mr. Samuel, 1790, Sturbridge, Massachusetts.

91

5.
Classroom Techniques

The simplicity of the rubbing technique allows even the very young student to become rapidly adept at reproducing surface and design elements. The teacher will be quick to realize there is little or no expense, no mess to clean up, and, most importantly, making rubbings is an excellent means through which many lessons can be introduced or reinforced. Rubbings made in the classroom and limited to pencil, chalk, or crayon are most practical.

In the primary grades a teacher can use rubbing as a way of introducing texture and tactile sensations. The making and collecting of rubbings of leaves, wood, flowers, grass, and stone might precede a simple science lesson. The lesson could be concluded by a "show and tell" session in which each child would be given an opportunity to speak about what he found and rubbed.

Children can make rubbings of foreign coins to enhance a geography project when the gluing of the original to the display is not convenient or practical. Field trips to historical places provide another excellent opportunity to make rubbings of signs, markers, placards or designs which cannot be removed or collected. And what better way is there to begin a unit on colonial America than by making, collecting, and displaying early gravestone rubbings?

Advanced science projects utilizing rubbings make eyecatching exhibits. Trees, leaves, flowers, some insects, sea plants, sponges, shells, and even several varieties of fishes can be rubbed.

The technique of rubbing is a boon to the art teacher, as it provides a simple, direct, and fast means of teaching so many things. Again, because of its simplicity, the technique of making rubbings is suitable for all grade levels. Texture and its two-dimensional counterpart, pattern, are the most obvious design elements to be illustrated by means of the rubbing process. In fact, almost every design and graphic element can be developed through the processes outlined in this book— among them, line, color, symmetrical and asymmetrical balance, repetitive design, variations on a theme, integration of shapes, positive and negative space, rhythm, and all aspects of composition.

Rubbing's close relationship to the other graphic arts makes it an excellent warm-up project for students intending to work in the more sophisticated print processes. There is, in fact, almost no difference between the printing and rubbing processes.

Difficult polychromatic prints are seldom made in the elementary grades. The teacher who wishes to introduce color may easily do so with rubbings. Rubbings can also be used as a means of allowing students to experiment with various media and techniques. A rubbing can be made with crayon and painted with an ink or watercolor wash; executed on Dayglow paper or with Dayglow crayons; cut and torn and pasted on a collage or combined with drawing, painting, and even sculpture. The rubbing is, perhaps, a universal instruction technique.

Making a rubbing of nylon mesh to use later as collage material.

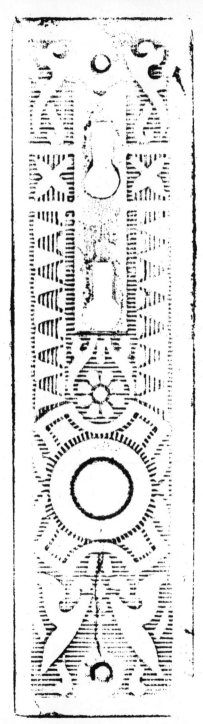

Rubbings made from
ornamental hardware using
pencil and tissue paper.

Opposite Page
Making a simple textured
rubbing to use in a collage.

Rubbings made from ornamental doorknobs
and coins with pencil and tissue paper.

Opposite Page
Making a simple rubbing from a metal trash basket.

Rubbing made from a glass doorknob.

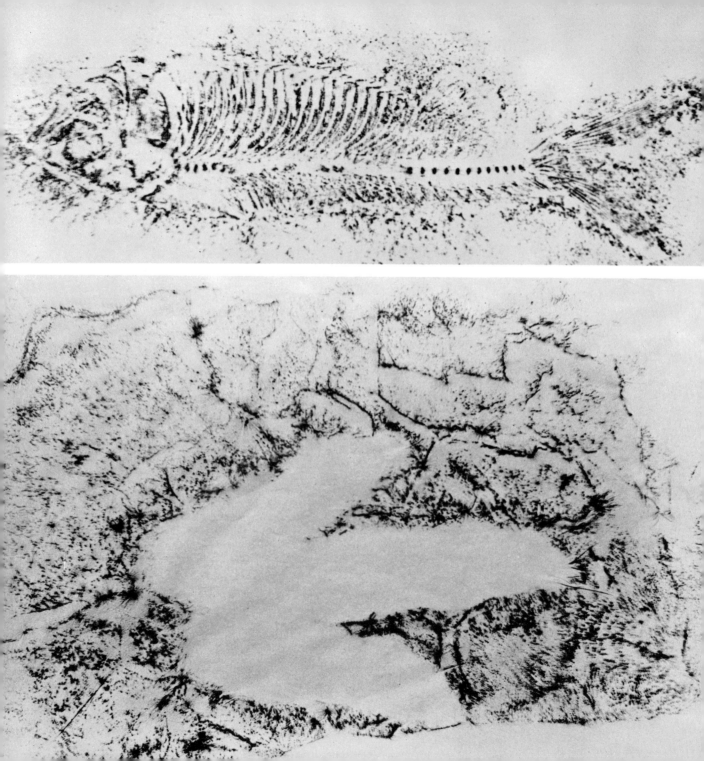

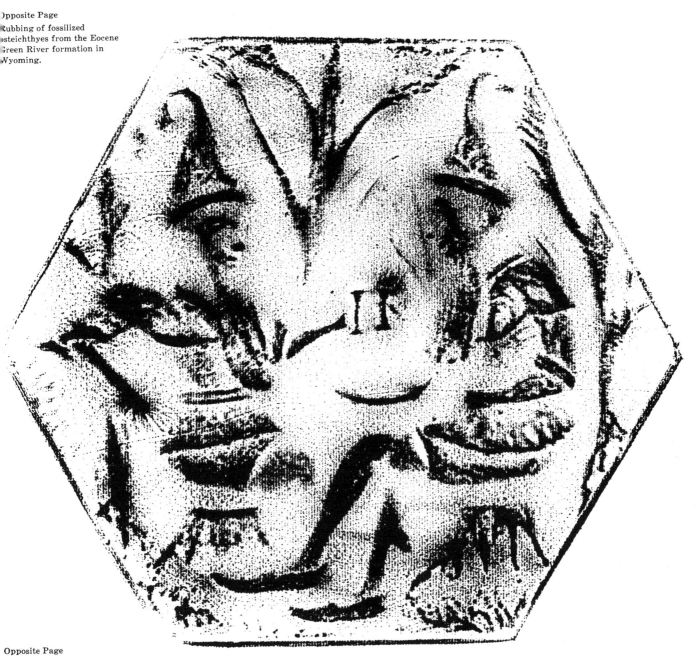

Rubbing made from a metal plaque.

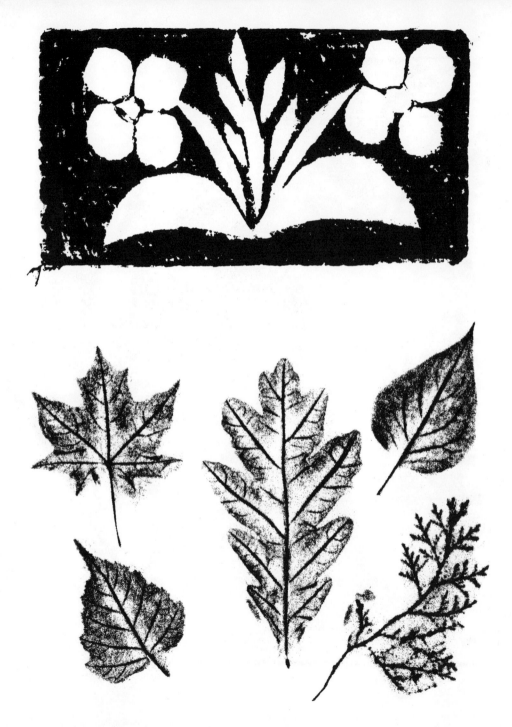

Rubbings using natural motifs—real and decorative leaves and flowers.

Technical Notes

Special Preparations

PLASTER—To mix plaster of paris, fill a rubber bowl half way with water. Applying Vaseline or a good hand cream will keep plaster from adhering to the hands. Sift the powder through the fingers into the water; never pour water into plaster of paris. As a general rule, bring the plaster almost to the water line before mixing it to get the correct consistency. If uncertain about the quantity needed, make the mixture thin. It will thicken with stirring. Do not stir the mixture until all the plaster is added. Once the plaster has been stirred, no more powder or water should be added. Stir by hand until all the lumps are dissolved and the mixture has a creamy consistency. It is now ready to use. Pour into the foil mold taking care to fill all the depressions, especially those along the edges. Allow to dry thoroughly before folding excess foil back.

METHYLCELLULOSE—Methylcellulose, used to adhere paper to a surface, can be purchased in three forms; tablet, powder, and liquid. Liquid methylcellulose can be used as is and requires no further preparation. Because of the difficulty in ordering, shipping, and storage, however, tablet or powder is preferred. Most drugstores carry methylcellulose under the brand name "Cellothyl," which is available in bottles of 100 0.5-gram tablets. When purchasing, request that the tablets be powdered. To use, mix about a level teaspoon of powder in one pint of warm water. The mixture must be shaken vigorously until all the methylcellulose is dissolved. This solution may have to be thickened or thinned depending on the weight of the paper; for this reason most people prefer to mix a thick stock solution and thin small quantities in a separate vessel to the correct consistency just before use. It is liberally applied to the paper with the fingers or elephant ear sponge.

LIVER OF SULPHUR—Depending on the supplier, liver of sulphur can be purchased in liquid, chunk or powder form. The liquid can be used as is, but warming slightly increases the speed at which a black patina is achieved. To prepare a liver of sulphur solution, mix powder or chunks with water. The dissolving of large chunks may be speeded by breaking them into smaller pieces with a hammer. A coffee or tobacco can can be used to contain the liquid if it is to be heated. Any heat source, stove, hot plate, or propane gas torch, can be used. It is advisable, however, to heat the mixture outside or in a well ventilated area, since the fumes given off during the process are extremely toxic. If done in a classroom, very strict supervision is necessary to prevent serious accidents. After the sulphur has become a solution the heat should be removed. The copper surface, cleaned with steel wool and Sparex, is washed with water and dried with a soft cloth. Paint on the liver of sulphur with a one-inch sash brush; the metal will turn black immediately. This can be washed and finished as explained in the chapter dealing with the foil technique or it may be repeated until the desired surface quality is achieved.

Cataloging, Storing, Displaying, and Photographing Rubbings

Cataloging—Rubbings taken from tombstones and monumental brasses are usually organized in one way or another. The simplest method is to group the rubbings alphabetically by church, county, town, or state. The information relating to each print is entered on an index card. This saves a great deal of wear and tear on the original. An acquisition number, dimensions, and the date may also be added.

Storing—Storing rubbings can be a problem. Those done in crayon or heelball will be affected by high temperatures and all are harmed by moisture. Small rubbings can be placed in a portfolio made from two pieces of corrugated cardboard taped at the bottom with cloth book-binding tape. Larger rubbings must be rolled, since folding detracts from the design and makes the print unsuitable for display. The rolls are best kept in cardboard mailing cylinders or those used for storing linoleum, oil cloth or fabrics. A piece of plastic held in place with a rubber band and placed over the ends of the tube keeps the rubbing clean. To avoid confusion each tube should be clearly labeled.

Displaying—Small rubbings can be matted and framed in the conventional way. Larger examples can be stretched over ¼-inch Upson board or Masonite. Because of the weight, these boards may have to be bolted to the wall. The use of glass is not practical on the larger rubbings. Spraying with a clear plastic fixative will offer some protection from the hazards of display. Ink rubbings can be pressed and dry mounted with photographic mounting tissue.

Photographing—Because of the difficulty in handling rubbings, many people photograph their work and file these pictures along with the index card. This is an excellent idea and averts many accidents in handling the originals.

To photograph a rubbing, tape the paper to a flat surface so that the wrinkles are eliminated. If the paper is very thin or torn, the underlying surface must be white or a dull gray photograph will result. The camera should be on a tripod and directly over or opposite the center of the surface to be copied. This is very important, for if the camera is not perpendicular to the rubbing, the edges of the print will be distorted and not square. A small opening or f-stop number must be used to prevent wrinkles from causing problems with depth of field and sharpness. Indoors, two lights of equal intensity should be aimed at the rubbing so as to meet at a 45-degree angle to the paper surface. If a "hot spot" of light is noticed it may be necessary to use a piece of cheese cloth or other such diffuser over both light sources. The larger the rubbing, the more difficult it is to light adequately.

If one does not wish to use lights, the photographs may be taken out-of-doors on a cloudy bright day. Direct sunlight is not desirable because it almost always causes a glare and dark shadows. If the photographs must be taken on such a day, the mounted rubbing should be placed in the open shade so that it is illuminated by reflected rather than direct sun light.

If the rubbing to be photographed is chiefly black and white, with little or no gray tones, the exposure or f number should be diminished by one stop. This over exposes the negative and will yield a print with rich blacks contrasted with an almost pure white. Often times stray marks and smudges will be so over exposed as not to register at all.

Many of the photographs in this book were made using the techniques above. The camera and lens contribute much to a fine photograph and should not be overlooked. All of the photographs by the author were taken with a 35mm single lens reflex camera and processed in his studio.

Bibliography

Burckhardt, E. *Chinesische Steinabreib-ungen.* Munich, 1961.

Capek, Abe. *Chinese Stone Pictures, a Distinctive Form of Chinese Art.* Spring Books, London, 1962.

Forbes, Harriette M. *Gravestones of Early New England.* Houghton Publishers, Boston, 1927.

Gillon, Edmund Vincent, Jr. *Early New England Gravestone Rubbings.* Dover Publications, Inc., N.Y., N.Y., 1966.

Haines, H. *A Manual of Monumental Brasses.* 2 vols. London, 1861.

Hempstead, Joshua. *The Diary of Joshua Hempstead.* Collections of the New London Historical Society, Connecticut, 1901.

Hiyama, Yoshio. *Gyotaku* (The Art and Technique of the Japanese Fish Print). Copyright by University of Tokyo Press, 1964. University of Washington Press, Seattle, Washington, 1964.

Ludwig, Allan. *Graven Images* (New England Stonecarving and its Symbols, 1650-1815). Wesleyan University Press, Middletown, Connecticut, 1966.

Ludwig, Allan. "Some Examples of Early New England Gravestones," *Graphis.* Zurich, Switzerland, 1963. Vol. 19, No. 108.

Ludwig, Allan. "Stonecarving in New England," *New Haven Colony Historical Society Journal.* New Haven, Connecticut, 1963. Vol. 12, No. 1.

Ludwig, Allan. "Stone Carving in New England Graveyards," *Antiques.* New York, 1964. Vol. LXXXVI, No. 1.

Ludwig, Janine Lowell. "The Forgotten Artists of Early America," *The New England Galaxy.* Sturbridge, Massachusetts, 1963. Vol. IV, No. 3.

Macklin, H. W. *The Brasses of England.* London, 1907.

Macklin, H. W. *Monumental Brasses.* Reprinted London, 1963.

Norris, Malcom. *Brass Rubbing.* Dover Publications, Inc., N.Y., N.Y. 1965.

Parker, Ann, and Avon Neal. *A Portfolio of Rubbings.* Elm Tree Press, Woodstock, Vermont, 1963.

Pommeranz-Liedtke, G. *Die Weisheit Der Kunst; Chinesische Steinabreibungen* (a portfolio of rubbings). Leipzig, 1965.

Speiser, Werner, et. al. *Chinese Art: Painting, Calligraphy, Stone Rubbing, Wood Engraving.* Universe Books, New York, 1964.

Stephenson, M. *A List of Monumental Brasses in the British Isles.* England, 1926. republished 1964.

Tze-yün, Ma and Yabuta Kaichirô. *Takubon no tsukurigata,* Kyôtô, 1963.

van Gulik, R. H. *Chinese Pictorial Art.* Rome, 1958.

Wallace, Charles A. *Stories on Stone.* New York, 1954.

Acknowledgments

I would like to express my appreciation and gratitude to the many individuals and organizations who helped with the preparation of this book. Among them especially:

The museums who permitted the use of reproductions of works from their collections and the library and photographic staffs of: The Seattle Art Museum, Seattle, Washington; The Metropolitan Museum of Art, New York; The Smithsonian Institution, Freer Gallery of Art, Washington, D.C.; The Cleveland Museum of Art, Cleveland, Ohio; The Baltimore Museum of Art, Baltimore, Maryland; The Fogg Art Museum, Harvard University, Cambridge, Massachusetts; The British Museum, London, England; The Homma Museum, Sakata Yamagata, Japan; and The Narodni Museum, Belgrade, Yugoslavia. The William H. Wolf, I.B.M., Meltzer, and Weyhe Galleries in New York for their interest in this book and for permitting the reproduction of photographs of rubbings in their collections; Dr. Hugo Munstenberg, professor of art history at the State University College at New Paltz, New York, for his invaluable assistance with the preliminary research for this book, his many perceptive comments and for permitting me to photograph rubbings in his collection; William B. Jones of New York, who first introduced me to the art of making rubbings of monumental brasses and for assisting me with my research in this area; Michael Black of Oxford, England, for supplying me with excellent reproductions of his rubbings of monumental brasses; Dr. Yoshio Hiyama, professor of fisheries biology, University of Tokyo, Tokyo, Japan, and author of the book *Gyotaku* (The Art of the Japanese Fish Print), for his information on the beginning of this technique in Japan and for permitting me to reproduce rubbings used in his book; Visit Srinava, Chief of the Tourist Organization of Thailand, New York, for granting me permission to photograph some of the rubbings he has made; Sally and Michael De Rosa of Pinebrook, New Jersey, for permitting me to photograph rubbings in their collection; Milos Nikolic of the Yugoslav Information Center in New York, without whose help the publication of the Serbian rubbings would have been impossible; Doubleday and Chanticleer Press, New York, for supplying me with their photograph of an ancestor plaque discovered in Taiwan; Ronald Januzzi, proprietor of the Dinosaur Track and Mineral Museum in Brewster, New York, for permitting rubbings to be taken from fossils in his collection; Ann Kepic for her help with the last minute correspondence; Steven Steinberg, manager of New York Central Supply, New York, for his assistance in evaluating and testing papers and other products necessary for making rubbings and for preparing a specialized catalog of these supplies; Mary Gale for typing and preparing the final manuscript for publication and for her editorial criticisms; Mitchell Siegel, Director of Art for the Ossining Public School System, Ossining, New York, for his active participation with this entire project; Betty McCue and Alice Watson, librarians for the Ossining Public School System, and Mrs. Max Faerber of Paragon Book Gallery, Ltd., New York for their assistance with the bibliographic research; the staff of the Reinhold Book Corporation for their personal interest in my work, notably Sterling McIlhany for his constant encouragement, perceptive criticisms, and enthusiastic support.